VERSANT ENGLISH SPEAKING VOICE TEST PRACTICE EXAMS WITH SAMPLE RESPONSES, FREE RECORDINGS, AND EXAM TIPS

The Versant Test and the Versant English Test are registered trademarks of Pearson, Inc, which is neither affiliated with nor endorses this publication.

Versant English Speaking Voice Test Practice Exams with Sample Responses, Free Recordings, and Exam Tips

© 2022 Test Prep Guides dba www.test-prep-guides.com

All rights reserved. No part of this publication may be reproduced, stored in a retrieval system, or transmitted, in any form or by any means, electronic, mechanical, photocopying, recording, or otherwise, without the prior written permission of the copyright owner.

ISBN: 978-1-949282-84-9

Note: The Versant Test and the Versant English Test are registered trademarks of Pearson, Inc, which is neither affiliated with nor endorses this publication.

TABLE OF CONTENTS

Versant English Speaking Practice Tests:

Practice Test 1	1
Part A – Reading Exercises and Tips	1
Part B – Repeat the Sentence Exercises and Tips	2
Part C – Answer the Question Exercises and Tips	2
Part D – Sentence Build Exercises and Tips	2
Part E – Story Retelling Examples and Tips	3
Part F – Open Questions Examples and Tips	4
Practice Test 2	5
Practice Test 3	7
Practice Test 4	9
Practice Test 5	11
Practice Test 6	13
Practice Test 7	15
Practice Test 8	17
Practice Test 9	19
Practice Test 10	21
Appendix 1 – Link to the Free MP3s	23
Appendix 2 – Useful Phrases	24
Answer Keys:	
Answers to Practice Test 1	26

Answers to Practice Test 2 — 35

Answers to Practice Test 3 — 44

Answers to Practice Test 4 — 53

Answers to Practice Test 5 — 62

Answers to Practice Test 6 — 71

Answers to Practice Test 7 — 80

Answers to Practice Test 8 — 89

Answers to Practice Test 9 — 98

Answers to Practice Test 10 — 107

VERSANT ENGLISH SPEAKING PRACTICE TEST 1

FOR INFORMATION ON HOW TO ACCESS THE SOUND FILES, PLEASE SEE APPENDIX 1.

Part A – Reading

Instructions: Open your test book to Part A of the practice exam. Read the sentences out loud when you hear the sentence number. You should stop speaking when you hear the beep. Note that on the real test, you will see the sentences on your computer screen.

Tips: On the real exam, you may not be asked to repeat all of the sentences. In addition, you may be asked to read the sentences in a non-sequential order, for example, sentence 8 and then sentence 3. You will see a button to click when you are ready to go to the next question. Read the sentence clearly with good pronunciation and with a reasonable speaking speed. To keep to a reasonable speed, try to repeat each sentence in these practice tests in the time allowed on the recordings.

1. Sam is a rancher in the west.
2. He owns a large ranch where he raises cows and horses.
3. He especially enjoys riding and training horses.
4. Every Saturday, children visit his ranch to see the animals.
5. Sally loves to travel internationally.
6. She has decided to look for work overseas.
7. She has a spirit of adventure and isn't afraid of change.
8. Fortunately, she managed to find work overseas as an English teacher.
9. Thomas's family members all work in the medical profession.
10. His mother is a doctor, and his father is a nurse.
11. They would like Thomas to be a pharmacist.
12. However, Thomas would like to be a lawyer.

Part B – Repeat

Instructions: Now you will hear 16 sentences. Repeat each sentence word-for-word.

Tips: Repeat each sentence as accurately as you can. You will need a good memory for this part of the exam. Improve your memorization skills by taking all of the practice tests in this book. Then listen to all of the Part B questions again as you look at the answers in the back of the book.

Part C – Questions

Instructions: Give a simple answer to each question. Your answer should be one to four words, rather than a full sentence.

Tips: You will usually have a fifty percent chance of getting a correct answer on this part of the test since, for many questions, you only need to repeat one of the two options provided. In the example below, the two options are a camera or a telephone, and you simply need to repeat the words "a telephone" for your response.

Example: Would you make a call with a camera or a telephone?

Answer: a telephone

Part D – Sentence Builds

Instructions: Rearrange the words or groups of words that you hear to form a question or sentence. Say your answer in the time provided on the recording.

Tips: Remember that some of the answers will be sentences, but others will be questions. When forming the questions, pay attention to the order of the verbs, as well as your intonation.

Example: over / get / here

Answer: Get over here!

Part E – Story Retelling

Instructions: Now you will hear three stories. You will hear each story once, followed by a beep. When you hear the beep, you will have 30 seconds to retell the story. Tell as much of the story as you can, including the names, action, and ending. You will hear another beep when the 30 seconds has finished.

Tips: Remember to include the following in your response – the person or people involved, the place, the event and the emotion about it, and the outcome or result.

Example:

Samira was really looking forward to her thirtieth birthday. She was going to have a party at her house and had invited friends and family members. Knowing there would be about fifty people there, she had even organized a catering company to prepare food. Then, Samira had an accident on her bike and got injured. She was in the hospital and had to cancel the party, so she was really disappointed about the situation.

People: Samira, her friends and family members

Place: Samira's house

Emotion or Event: birthday party; excitement, then disappointment

Outcome: party was canceled

Sample response:

Samira was so excited about her upcoming birthday. She was going to turn thirty and was planning a big party for her family and friends, and she even had plans for the catering. Then Samira had an accident on her bicycle, and she had to be hospitalized. She was so disappointed when she had to cancel the party.

Part F – Open Questions

Instructions: You will hear questions about family life or personal situations that are familiar to you. Each question will be spoken twice, followed by a beep. When you hear the beep, you will have 40 seconds to speak. You will hear another beep again at the end of the 40 seconds.

Tips: Remember to mention these points in your response – your opinion, examples or explanations, and any further information. Do not be concerned about the opinion that you express. You will be assessed on your language skills, not on your viewpoint.

Example:

Celebrities and famous athletes have a moral responsibility to children as role models. Do you agree? Please provide examples or explanations to support your viewpoint.

Your Opinion: I agree

Examples / Explanation: children copy behavior they see on social media

Further Information: celebrities should be careful about the example they make

Sample Response:

Celebrities and famous sports stars do indeed have a responsibility to young people as their role models. For example, children are often influenced by actions that they see on social media platforms, and they may even try to copy or imitate these behaviors because they admire these celebrities and want to be like them. In this case, celebrities should be mindful of their actions because, in my opinion, they are setting examples for young people.

VERSANT ENGLISH SPEAKING PRACTICE TEST 2

Part A – Reading

Instructions: Open your test book to Part A of the practice exam. Read the sentences out loud when you hear the sentence number. You should stop speaking when you hear the beep. Note that on the real test, you will see the sentences on your computer screen.

1. Larry is going to retire next month.

2. He has worked at the same company for 40 years.

3. He is looking forward to having time to himself to enjoy his hobbies.

4. His wife is hoping that they also can start to travel more

5. My co-worker keeps asking me for help with his tasks.

6. The situation is starting to distract me.

7. I need to pay attention to my job.

8. I think I am going to have to say something to my manager about it.

9. For her brother's birthday, Marta wanted to get him a new phone.

10. She realized that there were many different kinds of phones.

11. She was hoping to get her sister to help her choose one.

12. They ended up getting him one with many special features.

Part B – Repeat

Instructions: Now you will hear 16 sentences. Repeat each sentence word-for-word.

Part C – Questions

Instructions: Give a simple answer to each question. Your answer should be one to four words, rather than a full sentence.

Part D – Sentence Builds

Instructions: Rearrange the words or groups of words that you hear to form a question or sentence. Say your answer in the time provided on the recording.

Part E – Story Retelling

Instructions: Now you will hear three stories. You will hear each story once, followed by a beep. When you hear the beep, you will have 30 seconds to retell the story. Tell as much of the story as you can, including the names, action, and ending. You will hear another beep when the 30 seconds has finished.

Part F – Open Questions

Instructions: You will hear questions about family life or personal situations that are familiar to you. Each question will be spoken twice, followed by a beep. When you hear the beep, you will have 40 seconds to speak. You will hear another beep again at the end of the 40 seconds.

VERSANT ENGLISH SPEAKING PRACTICE TEST 3

Part A – Reading

Instructions: Open your test book to Part A of the practice exam. Read the sentences out loud when you hear the sentence number. You should stop speaking when you hear the beep. Note that on the real test, you will see the sentences on your computer screen.

1. Starting a new job can be really difficult.

2. You have to learn all of the new company policies.

3. You also have to learn the names of many new people.

4. Nonetheless, it is worth changing jobs in order to advance your career.

5. A lot of thought needs to go into buying a new car.

6. Some cars can be cheap to buy, but expensive to run.

7. Other cars might be more expensive, but run more efficiently.

8. So, a person should take enough time to consider all the options.

9. It can be wonderful to live in a warm, sunny climate.

10. The water in the sea can be ideal for swimming.

11. The beach can also be a nice place to relax.

12. In spite of this, care needs to be taken in order to avoid sun stroke.

Part B – Repeat

Instructions: Now you will hear 16 sentences. Repeat each sentence word-for-word.

Part C – Questions

Instructions: Give a simple answer to each question. Your answer should be one to four words, rather than a full sentence.

Part D – Sentence Builds

Instructions: Rearrange the words or groups of words that you hear to form a question or sentence. Say your answer in the time provided on the recording.

Part E – Story Retelling

Instructions: Now you will hear three stories. You will hear each story once, followed by a beep. When you hear the beep, you will have 30 seconds to retell the story. Tell as much of the story as you can, including the names, action, and ending. You will hear another beep when the 30 seconds has finished.

Part F – Open Questions

Instructions: You will hear questions about family life or personal situations that are familiar to you. Each question will be spoken twice, followed by a beep. When you hear the beep, you will have 40 seconds to speak. You will hear another beep again at the end of the 40 seconds.

VERSANT ENGLISH SPEAKING PRACTICE TEST 4

Part A – Reading

Instructions: Open your test book to Part A of the practice exam. Read the sentences out loud when you hear the sentence number. You should stop speaking when you hear the beep. Note that on the real test, you will see the sentences on your computer screen.

1. Heavy traffic is a big problem in New York City.//
2. It can be especially difficult to travel around Central Park.
3. Vans and trucks that are making deliveries can also cause problems.
4. For these reasons, many people prefer to travel on the subway.
5. Bill was late for work every day last week.
6. His boss warned him that if he was late again, he might lose his job.
7. Bill decided he had better start to set his alarm clock a half an hour earlier.
8. He now manages to get to work on time every day.
9. Anna is studying to take her driver's test.
10. She really needs to drive in order to get into work.
11. She has to take a written exam, and then drive the car for a practical exam.
12. She is getting really nervous about the whole experience.

Part B – Repeat

Instructions: Now you will hear 16 sentences. Repeat each sentence word-for-word.

Part C – Questions

Instructions: Give a simple answer to each question. Your answer should be one to four words, rather than a full sentence.

Part D – Sentence Builds

Instructions: Rearrange the words or groups of words that you hear to form a question or sentence. Say your answer in the time provided on the recording.

Part E – Story Retelling

Instructions: Now you will hear three stories. You will hear each story once, followed by a beep. When you hear the beep, you will have 30 seconds to retell the story. Tell as much of the story as you can, including the names, action, and ending. You will hear another beep when the 30 seconds has finished.

Part F – Open Questions

Instructions: You will hear questions about family life or personal situations that are familiar to you. Each question will be spoken twice, followed by a beep. When you hear the beep, you will have 40 seconds to speak. You will hear another beep again at the end of the 40 seconds.

VERSANT ENGLISH SPEAKING PRACTICE TEST 5

Part A – Reading

Instructions: Open your test book to Part A of the practice exam. Read the sentences out loud when you hear the sentence number. You should stop speaking when you hear the beep. Note that on the real test, you will see the sentences on your computer screen.

1. Football players often suffer from frequent injuries.
2. Knee and shoulder injuries are among the most common.
3. They often need to have surgery at one time or another.
4. Some players need to retire early because they are no longer able to play.
5. Mike's next-door neighbors are really noisy.
6. They play loud music at all-night parties on the weekends.
7. Mike is finding it really hard to sleep.
8. He is thinking of filing a complaint about them with the city.
9. Employees are allowed to have a free lunch and a free supper.
10. Lunches usually include sandwiches and a juice or drink.
11. Suppers are normally hot meals.
12. These free meals are an important employee benefit.

Part B – Repeat

Instructions: Now you will hear 16 sentences. Repeat each sentence word-for-word.

Part C – Questions

Instructions: Give a simple answer to each question. Your answer should be one to four words, rather than a full sentence.

Part D – Sentence Builds

Instructions: Rearrange the words or groups of words that you hear to form a question or sentence. Say your answer in the time provided on the recording.

Part E – Story Retelling

Instructions: Now you will hear three stories. You will hear each story once, followed by a beep. When you hear the beep, you will have 30 seconds to retell the story. Tell as much of the story as you can, including the names, action, and ending. You will hear another beep when the 30 seconds has finished.

Part F – Open Questions

Instructions: You will hear questions about family life or personal situations that are familiar to you. Each question will be spoken twice, followed by a beep. When you hear the beep, you will have 40 seconds to speak. You will hear another beep again at the end of the 40 seconds.

VERSANT ENGLISH SPEAKING PRACTICE TEST 6

Part A – Reading

Instructions: Open your test book to Part A of the practice exam. Read the sentences out loud when you hear the sentence number. You should stop speaking when you hear the beep. Note that on the real test, you will see the sentences on your computer screen.

1. Linda is thinking of buying a new house.
2. She has been living in a small apartment.
3. She is looking forward to getting out of the city.
4. On the other hand, she is not excited about having to drive to work.
5. Frank really enjoys traveling, especially overseas.
6. He has already traveled through all of Europe and most of South America.
7. He is hoping to go to Africa next.
8. However, he needs to get his passport renewed before his next trip.
9. Berta was hoping to become a nurse one day.
10. She studied science at school and volunteered at the local hospital.
11. Then, she realized that she didn't like the sight of blood.
12. She decided to become a computer programmer instead.

Part B – Repeat

Instructions: Now you will hear 16 sentences. Repeat each sentence word-for-word.

Part C – Questions

Instructions: Give a simple answer to each question. Your answer should be one to four words, rather than a full sentence.

Part D – Sentence Builds

Instructions: Rearrange the words or groups of words that you hear to form a question or sentence. Say your answer in the time provided on the recording.

Part E – Story Retelling

Instructions: Now you will hear three stories. You will hear each story once, followed by a beep. When you hear the beep, you will have 30 seconds to retell the story. Tell as much of the story as you can, including the names, action, and ending. You will hear another beep when the 30 seconds has finished.

Part F – Open Questions

Instructions: You will hear questions about family life or personal situations that are familiar to you. Each question will be spoken twice, followed by a beep. When you hear the beep, you will have 40 seconds to speak. You will hear another beep again at the end of the 40 seconds.

VERSANT ENGLISH SPEAKING PRACTICE TEST 7

Part A – Reading

Instructions: Open your test book to Part A of the practice exam. Read the sentences out loud when you hear the sentence number. You should stop speaking when you hear the beep. Note that on the real test, you will see the sentences on your computer screen.

1. Today is Emily's 90th birthday.

2. Her grandchildren are going to come visit her.

3. They are going to bring a special birthday cake.

4. It should be a very happy day.

5. Emma works in a busy call center in customer service.

6. Her co-worker keeps trying to talk to her when she is on the phone.

7. She is finding it difficult to hear what the customers are saying.

8. After two days of frustration, she decided to tell her boss about it.

9. Louise purchased a new sofa at the furniture store.

10. On the day that it was delivered, she realized that it was damaged.

11. She called the company to ask for a replacement.

12. The replacement is going to be delivered next week.

Part B – Repeat

Instructions: Now you will hear 16 sentences. Repeat each sentence word-for-word.

Part C – Questions

Instructions: Give a simple answer to each question. Your answer should be one to four words, rather than a full sentence.

Part D – Sentence Builds

Instructions: Rearrange the words or groups of words that you hear to form a question or sentence. Say your answer in the time provided on the recording.

Part E – Story Retelling

Instructions: Now you will hear three stories. You will hear each story once, followed by a beep. When you hear the beep, you will have 30 seconds to retell the story. Tell as much of the story as you can, including the names, action, and ending. You will hear another beep when the 30 seconds has finished.

Part F – Open Questions

Instructions: You will hear questions about family life or personal situations that are familiar to you. Each question will be spoken twice, followed by a beep. When you hear the beep, you will have 40 seconds to speak. You will hear another beep again at the end of the 40 seconds.

VERSANT ENGLISH SPEAKING PRACTICE TEST 8

Part A – Reading

Instructions: Open your test book to Part A of the practice exam. Read the sentences out loud when you hear the sentence number. You should stop speaking when you hear the beep. Note that on the real test, you will see the sentences on your computer screen.

1. Moving to a new city can be a lonely experience.
2. A person might be busy at work, but feel lonely in the evenings.
3. It can also be difficult to learn how to travel into the city center.
4. For this reason, some people prefer to stay close to their hometowns.
5. Buying a pet can be a big commitment.
6. First, a person needs to decide what kind of pet they would like.
7. Pet food can be costly, and the vet can also be expensive.
8. Nevertheless, owing a pet can really enhance a person's life.
9. Some people feel depressed when it rains.
10. During rainy days, it can be difficult to get outdoors.
11. Poor weather can also limit a person's exercise.
12. Because of this, some people prefer to join a gym.

Part B – Repeat

Instructions: Now you will hear 16 sentences. Repeat each sentence word-for-word.

Part C – Questions

Instructions: Give a simple answer to each question. Your answer should be one to four words, rather than a full sentence.

Part D – Sentence Builds

Instructions: Rearrange the words or groups of words that you hear to form a question or sentence. Say your answer in the time provided on the recording.

Part E – Story Retelling

Instructions: Now you will hear three stories. You will hear each story once, followed by a beep. When you hear the beep, you will have 30 seconds to retell the story. Tell as much of the story as you can, including the names, action, and ending. You will hear another beep when the 30 seconds has finished.

Part F – Open Questions

Instructions: You will hear questions about family life or personal situations that are familiar to you. Each question will be spoken twice, followed by a beep. When you hear the beep, you will have 40 seconds to speak. You will hear another beep again at the end of the 40 seconds.

VERSANT ENGLISH SPEAKING PRACTICE TEST 9

Part A – Reading

Instructions: Open your test book to Part A of the practice exam. Read the sentences out loud when you hear the sentence number. You should stop speaking when you hear the beep. Note that on the real test, you will see the sentences on your computer screen.

1. Visiting the mountains is a wonderful experience.
2. Because of the snow, the air feels cold and fresh.
3. Some people even like to go hiking in the snow.
4. But personally, I would rather stay inside by a warm fire.
5. Denise has a full-time job as a legal assistant.
6. She works in a law office for a criminal attorney.
7. In the evenings, she attends classes at a local university.
8. She is studying to become a lawyer herself.
9. Management-level positions come with a great deal of responsibility.
10. Managers not only need to supervise staff.
11. They also need to prepare reports and a lot of paperwork.
12. Although these tasks can be difficult, the higher salary compensates for this.

Part B – Repeat

Instructions: Now you will hear 16 sentences. Repeat each sentence word-for-word.

Part C – Questions

Instructions: Give a simple answer to each question. Your answer should be one to four words, rather than a full sentence.

Part D – Sentence Builds

Instructions: Rearrange the words or groups of words that you hear to form a question or sentence. Say your answer in the time provided on the recording.

Part E – Story Retelling

Instructions: Now you will hear three stories. You will hear each story once, followed by a beep. When you hear the beep, you will have 30 seconds to retell the story. Tell as much of the story as you can, including the names, action, and ending. You will hear another beep when the 30 seconds has finished.

Part F – Open Questions

Instructions: You will hear questions about family life or personal situations that are familiar to you. Each question will be spoken twice, followed by a beep. When you hear the beep, you will have 40 seconds to speak. You will hear another beep again at the end of the 40 seconds.

VERSANT ENGLISH SPEAKING PRACTICE TEST 10

Part A – Reading

Instructions: Open your test book to Part A of the practice exam. Read the sentences out loud when you hear the sentence number. You should stop speaking when you hear the beep. Note that on the real test, you will see the sentences on your computer screen.

1. Jenny enjoys playing golf with her friends.

2. She especially likes to play on the weekends.

3. Her husband got her a golf cart as a surprise.

4. She likes using it to get around the golf course.

5. Insects are quite helpful, although many people are afraid of them.

6. Bees help many different kinds of plants to grow.

7. Spiders also help to control other insects.

8. On the other hand, some bugs spread diseases.

9. Working as an emergency surgeon is a high-pressure job.

10. It can take more than ten years of training to get a job.

11. The outcome of operations is usually a matter of life or death.

12. Therefore, this profession attracts only a certain type of person.

Part B – Repeat

Instructions: Now you will hear 16 sentences. Repeat each sentence word-for-word.

Part C – Questions

Instructions: Give a simple answer to each question. Your answer should be one to four words, rather than a full sentence.

Part D – Sentence Builds

Instructions: Rearrange the words or groups of words that you hear to form a question or sentence. Say your answer in the time provided on the recording.

Part E – Story Retelling

Instructions: Now you will hear three stories. You will hear each story once, followed by a beep. When you hear the beep, you will have 30 seconds to retell the story. Tell as much of the story as you can, including the names, action, and ending. You will hear another beep when the 30 seconds has finished.

Part F – Open Questions

Instructions: You will hear questions about family life or personal situations that are familiar to you. Each question will be spoken twice, followed by a beep. When you hear the beep, you will have 40 seconds to speak. You will hear another beep again at the end of the 40 seconds.

APPENDIX 1

For the audio recordings that accompany these practice tests, please go to:

https://test-prep-guides.com/versant-test-practice-online/english-speaking-exam/

APPENDIX 2

More Useful Phrases for the Test

This section contains useful phrases for Part F of the exam. The phrases have been placed into categories, according to the functions that you will need to use on the test. You should study the following lists and try to use these words as you respond to the sample exercises in this book. In addition, study the underlined phrases in the sample responses for Part F in the answer key that follows.

Phrases for talking about the present

at present

at the moment

every day

nowadays

right now

so far

until now

Phrases for collecting your thoughts

Anyway, . . .

As I said before, . . .

As I was saying, . . .

In any event, . . .

So, . . .

The thing is . . .

Well . . .

What I am trying to say is that . . .

Phrases for emphasizing

Actually, . . .

In fact, . . .

The fact is that . . .

To be honest, . . .

. . . really . . .

Phrases for explaining what you mean

I mean, . . .

I mean that . . .

In other words, . . .

What I mean is . . .

Phrases for giving examples

For example, . . .

For instance, . . .

In particular, . . .

Phrases for giving generalizations

as a rule

for the most part

generally speaking

in general

in most cases

on the whole

ANSWER KEYS

Answers to Practice Test 1

Part B – Repeat

1. It is winter, and it is very cold.

2. I like to travel alone because it's so much easier.

3. Could you please be quiet?

4. What a boring movie!

5. Have you ever gone camping?

6. He had a horrible accident in his car.

7. It looks like tomorrow will be nice and sunny.

8. Aren't we supposed to have a meeting today?

9. Well, you never said you needed help, did you?

10. I'm hungry. Could you get me something to eat please?

11. I'm going to a conference tomorrow. I can't say I'm looking forward to it though.

12. I didn't get a raise because the boss said the company is making cut backs.

13. Would you mind if I borrowed your laptop for a couple of days?

14. Companies can spend huge amounts of money on marketing campaigns.

15. I'm busy, so if you could leave me alone, I'd appreciate it.

16. Gossiping about others can be harmful to their reputations.

Answers to Practice Test 1

Part C – Questions

1. Would you take a drink from a plate or a glass? **a glass**

2. How many hours are there in a day? **twenty-four**

3. Which one has fur, a rabbit or a snake? **a rabbit**

4. What do you call the outer part of a sandwich? **bread / slices of bread**

5. Would you go to sleep in a desk or in a bed? **in a bed**

6. Which is sweet, honey or water? **honey**

7. Which is smaller, an elephant or a cat? **a cat**

8. Do babies crawl or walk? **crawl**

9. Who is your father's mother? **your grandmother**

10. Do dogs have two legs or four? **four**

11. Does the desert have sand or grass? **grass**

12. How many wheels does a bicycle have? **two**

13. Which is heavier, a table or a car? **a car**

14. What do you call a baby dog? **a puppy**

15. Which comes first, twenty-one or fifty-four? **twenty-one**

16. Which is darker, black or white? **black**

17. How many sides are in a triangle? **three**

18. What would you put on your feet, shoes or shirts? **shoes**

19. What would you call the husband of a queen? **a king**

20. What language is spoken in France? **French**

21. What do you call the vehicle that collects injured people? **an ambulance**

22. How many seconds are in a minute? **sixty**

23. Which one is hotter, boiling or freezing? **boiling**

24. How many legs does a person have? **two**

25. To eat, do you use your mouth or ears? **your mouth**

Answers to Practice Test 1

Part D – Sentence Builds

1. at 10 o'clock / to my house / come

   Come to my house at 10 o'clock.

2. quickly / two huge hamburgers / he ate

   He ate two huge hamburgers quickly.

3. a dog house / in the garden / they built

   They built a dog house in the garden.

4. this letter / head office / was sent by

   This letter was sent by head office.

5. start / I really should / exercising more

   I really should start exercising more.

6. the one / your friend was / who got sick

   Your friend was the one who got sick.

7. whether our customers / I don't know / will like it

   I don't know whether our customers will like it.

8. arrived late / you sent / the letter

   The letter you sent arrived late.

9. with what / I don't agree / he said

   I don't agree with what he said.

10. leave the documents / could you / with my assistant

    Could you leave the documents with my assistant?

Answers to Practice Test 1

Part E – Story Retelling

Passage 1:

Samantha had a job answering phone calls in a customer service center. After doing the job for seven years, she felt like she needed a change. So she took a long vacation to think about her situation. She decided to change careers, and went back to college to become a nurse.

Person: Samantha

Place: customer service center

Emotion or Event: tired, needed change

Outcome: decided to become a nurse

Sample Response 1:

Samantha was working in a call center answering calls from customers all day long, but she decided it might be time to change jobs. She went on a vacation to have some time to think about things. While on her vacation, she made the decision to return to further education to get training as a nurse.

Answers to Practice Test 1

Part E – Story Retelling

Passage 2:

Bart was watching a scary movie at his house with a friend. After they had been watching the movie for about twenty minutes, they heard a sound like a gunshot outside. They called the police to report the problem, but when the police arrived, they discovered that the noise had just come from an old car.

Person: Bart and his friend

Place: Bart's house

Emotion or Event: scary, afraid

Outcome: called police, but just an old car

Sample Response 2:

Bart and a friend of his were at Bart's house watching a scary movie. They had been watching the movie for a little while, when they heard a loud noise outside that sounded like a gun. They decided to call the police, but when the police got there, they determined that the noise was only from an old car.

Answers to Practice Test 1

Part E – Story Retelling

Passage 3:

Emelia was taking her dog for a walk in the city park when she discovered a cat under a tree. The cat was all alone and looked abandoned and hungry. Emelia decided to take the cat home with her, and she put information on social media about the lost cat. After a year, no one had claimed the cat, and it still lives with Emelia.

Person: Emelia

Place: city park

Emotion or Event: felt sorry for the cat

Outcome: tried to find owner, cat lives with her

Sample Response 3:

Emelia was walking in the city park one day with her dog when she found an abandoned and starving cat under a tree. Emelia felt sorry for the cat, so she took it home with her and tried to find the owner. She put up notices about the cat on social media, but a year later, no owner had come forward. So the cat lives with Emelia now.

Answers to Practice Test 1

Part F – Open Questions

Question 1:

Does the internet have a positive or negative effect on our lives? Please explain your answer.

Your Opinion: both positive and negative

Examples / Explanation: educational material; inappropriate dangerous material

Further Information: pornography; encouragement of suicide or eating disorders

Sample Response:

In my opinion, the internet has both positive and negative aspects. The internet has a great deal of educational and informative material that can help us with daily tasks. However, there is also inappropriate and even dangerous information online, such as pornography or publications that encourage suicide or eating disorders. Therefore, information on the internet needs to be used carefully and with a critical mind.

Useful phrases:

In my opinion, the internet has both positive and negative aspects. The internet has a great deal of educational and informative material that can help us with daily tasks. However, there is also inappropriate and even dangerous information online, such as pornography or publications that encourage suicide or eating disorders. Therefore, information on the internet needs to be used carefully and with a critical mind.

Answers to Practice Test 1

Part F – Open Questions

Question 2:

Is it better to live in a city or in the countryside? Please explain your answer.

Your Opinion: countryside

Examples / Explanation: relaxing, less pollution, noise, and crowding

Further Information: but some people prefer the active life of the city

Sample Response:

For me, a life in the countryside would just be ideal. When a person is in the country surrounded by nature, there is always a feeling of tranquility and relaxation. In environments away from the city, there is also less pollution and noise, as well as fewer crowds. In spite of these disadvantages, it is understandable that some people prefer the amenities and activities that can be found in city living.

Useful Phrases:

<u>For me</u>, a life in the countryside would just be ideal. When a person is in the country surrounded by nature, <u>there is always</u> a feeling of tranquility and relaxation. In environments away from the city, <u>there is also</u> less pollution and noise, as well as fewer crowds. <u>In spite of these disadvantages</u>, <u>it is understandable that</u> some people prefer the amenities and activities that can be found in city living.

Answers to Practice Test 2

Part B – Repeat

1. You can adjust it, according to your preference.

2. Why am I always in the bath when the telephone rings?

3. For the news report, tune in at 5:30.

4. We really should invite Scarlet to the party.

5. That's not a pizza. It's a cheese sandwich.

6. Henry is back home now after his vacation.

7. Before you sit down, please pick up your name tag.

8. Do you feel like coming out to dinner with us?

9. You will need photo identification to register for the test.

10. There has been a leak below the sink for quite a few days.

11. Go right at the second corner after the bank.

12. Do you have any other monthly plans that are less expensive?

13. The company decided to open an office in town.

14. Somebody will have to pay for the damage.

15. Your ideas are unique, but I don't think they'll be accepted.

16. If you want to send mail overseas for the holidays, you should do so before December 5th.

Answers to Practice Test 2

Part C – Questions

1. What do we call a baby boy who has become an adult?   **a man**

2. Is singing something musical or scientific? **musical**

3. Do you usually go more slowly on foot or on a train? **on foot**

4. What would you use to clean your teeth, a toothbrush or a stone? **a toothbrush**

5. Would you put gloves on your hands or feet?   **on your hands**

6. What would you use to go swimming, a bathing suit or jeans? **a bathing suit**

7. Would a spectator or a witness attend a football game? **a spectator**

8. Is a beach covered with paint or with sand? **with sand**

9. Is water that flows through the countryside a river or an ocean? **a river**

10. Is a hurricane a kind of storm or a type of food?   **a kind of storm**

11. If I'm told to hang on, should I wait or leave? **wait**

12. Would you find buttons on a shirt or on a book? **on a shirt**

13. What tool would you use to measure something, a hammer or a ruler? **a ruler**

14. To enter a museum, would you buy a ticket or a sandwich? **a ticket / buy a ticket**

15. David has become slim. Is he fat or thin? **thin**

16. Timothy is four years older than Lucie. She is 18. How old is Timothy?

   twenty-two

17. Would you find a desk in an office or in the forest? **in an office**

18. Isabel ate up the information. Did she pay attention or act bored?

   She paid attention.

19. Which could be used to make a bag, cloth or wood? **cloth**

20. The couple broke up. Are they together or separate? **separate**

21. Are hamburgers made from meat or from fabric? **from meat**

22. If Mark was furious, was he upset or relaxed? **upset**

23. The couple reconciled after their argument. Did they make up or end the

   relationship? **They made up.**

24. You need to look after a friend's dog. Are you going to feed it or ignore it?

   feed it

25. Which would you usually wear in the rain, a jacket or a gown? **a jacket**

Answers to Practice Test 2

Part D – Sentence Builds

1. finish / let's / this project

    Let's finish this project.

2. put / on the desk / that report

    Put that report on the desk.

3. speaking / the boss / continued

    The boss continued speaking

4. had often / she / been there

    She had often been there.

5. I can / the best that / I'm trying

    I'm trying the best that I can.

6. a meal / at the restaurant / she ate

    She ate a meal at the restaurant.

7. can sometimes / movies and shows / be scary

    Movies and shows can sometimes be scary.

8. that he was going to / the man said / arrive late

    The man said that he was going to arrive late.

9. to remain silent / told him / his lawyer

    His lawyer told him to remain silent.

10. she couldn't understand / was broken / why her computer

    She couldn't understand why her computer was broken.

Answers to Practice Test 2

Part E – Story Retelling

Passage 1:

Harriet and William had been married for ten years. They decided to spend a weekend at a cabin at the lake to celebrate their anniversary. They had really been looking forward to it, but it was a cold weekend with no sun. In the end, they had to stay inside the cabin all weekend.

Person: Harriet and William

Place: a cabin

Emotion or Event: excitement, looking forward

Outcome: bad weather, stayed inside

Sample Response 1:

Harriet and William decided to have a get-away at a cabin in order to celebrate their tenth wedding anniversary. They had been looking forward to it, but in the end, the weather wasn't great; it was a bit cold and the sun didn't come out at all. So they stayed in their cabin the whole weekend.

Answers to Practice Test 2

Part E – Story Retelling

Passage 2:

Mr. Smith was a coach for the football team at the local high school. His team had a big game on the weekend for the championship. Mr. Smith set his alarm clock to be sure to arrive at school on time for the game, but his clock didn't work. When he didn't show up at school on the morning of the game, one of his students had to go to his house to wake him up.

Person: Mr. Smith (a coach)

Place: his house

Emotion or Event: tired; championship game

Outcome: student went to his house to get him up

Sample Response 2:

Mr. Smith was a coach for the local football team. The team had a big match on the weekend, so the coach set his alarm to get up early the next day. However, there was a problem with his alarm, and it didn't go off. In the end, a student had to go to the coach's house to get him up.

Answers to Practice Test 2

Part E – Story Retelling

Passage 3:

Nathan and Becky were going to get married at the end of the month. Before the wedding, they decided to take dance classes, so they could do a special wedding dance for their guests. All of the guests really loved the dance, and many of them decided to take dance lessons themselves after the wedding.

Person: Nathan and Becky

Place: their wedding

Emotion or Event: love

Outcome: they danced; others decided to learn to dance

Sample Response 3:

Nathan and Becky were going to get married in a month, and they decided to learn how to dance in order to do a dance at their wedding. On the day of the wedding, the guests loved the dance, and many guests said that they were going to take dance classes themselves.

Answers to Practice Test 2

Part F – Open Questions

Question 1:

Which job would you rather have, one that is indoors or one that is outdoors? Explain why.

Your Opinion: indoors

Examples / Explanation: professional office, predictable, no bad weather

Further Information: some jobs must be done outdoors

Sample Response:

Personally, I prefer working indoors simply because of the predictability of the situation. When a person works indoors, one does not have to think about things like the heat or poor weather that really have a huge impact when working outdoors. I also enjoy the steady rhythm of a professional office job. It must be said though, that certain jobs have to be done outside, and I am grateful for the people that do those jobs.

Useful Phrases:

<u>Personally</u>, <u>I prefer</u> working indoors simply because of the predictability of the situation. <u>When a person</u> works indoors, one does not have to think about things like the heat or poor weather that really <u>have a huge impact</u> when working outdoors. <u>I also enjoy</u> the steady rhythm of a professional office job. <u>It must be said though</u>, that certain jobs have to be done outside, and I am grateful for the people that do those jobs.

Answers to Practice Test 2

Part F – Open Questions

Question 2:

Is new technology, like smart phones and other devices, good or bad for us? Why or why not?

Your Opinion: both good and bad

Examples / Explanation: better communication and navigation

Further Information: social media addiction

Sample Response:

Like most things in life, smart phones have both advantages and disadvantages. It is great to use a smart phone to communicate with friends or to find directions to navigate to unknown places. Yet, I would say that some people do indeed rely upon their devices too much, to the point that they even get a bit addicted to them. Social media is probably one of the biggest reasons for this phenomenon.

Useful Phrases:

<u>Like most things in life,</u> smart phones <u>have both advantages and disadvantages</u>. <u>It is great to</u> use a smart phone to communicate with friends or to find directions to navigate to unknown places. <u>Yet, I would say that</u> some people do indeed rely upon their devices too much, <u>to the point that</u> they even get a bit addicted to them. Social media is probably one of the biggest reasons for this phenomenon.

Answers to Practice Test 3

Part B – Repeat

1. Could I get this in a larger size?
2. Employees should contact Brad for more information.
3. We are hoping to buy a house next month.
4. It takes ten days for the item to be delivered.
5. We need to ask Madison to help us with this.
6. My sister's house is on the south side of the city.
7. Could I please join the English class that meets on Tuesday evening?
8. Customers are entitled to make returns for 28 days after purchase.
9. Go through the main door and then open the door on the left.
10. Everyone else had gone home, but Monica took no notice.
11. The waves came in as the boat went by the dock.
12. His flight for London leaves at 9:30 PM.
13. If you pay after the fifth, late charges will be added.
14. You can see a great view of the mountains from the balcony.
15. Many different kinds of classes are available at the local college.
16. I enjoyed looking around, even though I had no intention of buying anything.

Answers to Practice Test 3

Part C – Questions

1. The game has been called off. Have they played or has it been canceled?

    canceled

2. Can you drink juice or cake? **juice**

3. What item would you use to cut food, a suitcase or a knife? **a knife**

4. When Reese cleaned the clothes, did she wash them or iron them? **wash them**

5. What day of the week comes before Friday and after Wednesday? **Thursday**

6. How many minutes are there in half an hour? **thirty**

7. Does an outgoing person probably have a few friends or many friends? **many friends**

8. If you let an employee go, do you hire or fire them? **fire them**

9. Who would you ask to mow your grass, a gardener or an engineer? **a gardener**

10. Is something economical usually cheap or expensive? **cheap**

11. Carter just got a promotion. Is his boss happy or unhappy with his work? **happy**

12. If you want to send email, would you use a computer or a magazine? **a computer**

13. Janice was laid off. Is she working or is she unemployed? **unemployed**

14. Bailey is going to cook meat for the barbeque. Will he wear an apron or mittens?

    an apron

15. Would Faith play a piano with her hands or elbows? **her hands**

16. Ezra feels too cold. Should he light a fire or open the window? **light a fire**

17. When a person tells you something in confidence, is it well-known or a secret? **a secret**

18. That snake is poisonous. Is it dangerous or harmless? **dangerous**

19. What would you use to clean the window, a sponge or a shovel? **a sponge**

20. You have ordered a frozen milkshake. Is it warm or cold? **cold**

21. If I have my head buried in a book, am I reading or sleeping? **reading**

22. If Easton's floor is flooded, does he need a mop or a fork? **a mop**

23. I am not clear about the explanation. Have I understood or am I confused?

    confused

24. What organ in the human body is used for breathing, the lungs or the stomach?

    the lungs

25. You need to bring something up at the meeting tomorrow. Should you speak or be silent? **You should speak.**

Answers to Practice Test 3

Part D – Sentence Builds

1. getting used to / she was / her new job

    She was getting used to her new job.

2. forever / ignore it / you can't

    You can't ignore it forever.

3. the hotel / on the weekend / is busy

    The hotel is busy on the weekend. / On the weekend, the hotel is busy.

4. before / been a problem / there has never

    There has never been a problem before.

5. a raise / last week / I was given

    I was given a raise last week. / Last week, I was given a raise.

6. you can / your password / easily change

    You can easily change your password.

7. on Monday / will be finished / the project

    The project will be finished on Monday. / On Monday, the project will be finished.

8. a new car / to have bought / they seem

    They seem to have bought a new car.

9. with something dirty / was covered / the floor

    The floor was covered with something dirty.

10. to hear / everyone wanted / about the news

    Everyone wanted to hear about the news.

Answers to Practice Test 3

Part E – Story Retelling

Passage 1:

Carl is the owner of a technology business, and he frequently needs to fly to meetings in other countries. He had a big trip planned for an important meeting in the north of England. However, when he arrived at the airport, he was informed that it was snowing heavily there, and the flight was canceled.

Person: Carl, technology business owner

Place: north of England

Emotion or Event: flies to meeting abroad

Outcome: snowing; flight canceled

Sample Response 1:

Carl is a technology-business owner who often has to fly abroad for business meetings. He had an important meeting scheduled in the north of England, but when he got to the airport to fly to the UK, it was snowing there, and he was told that the flight was canceled.

Answers to Practice Test 3

Part E – Story Retelling

Passage 2:

The family next door has a new baby named David. The baby is normally very quiet, but he cries quite loudly whenever he gets hungry. One night, the father made a bottle of milk for David, but he didn't like it because it was too hot. The father added some cold water, and the baby drank the whole bottle and went to sleep.

Person: family and baby David

Place: next door

Emotion or Event: bottle of milk too hot

Outcome: added cold water; baby drank it and went to sleep

Sample Response 2:

Next door, there is a family that has a new baby. The name of the baby is David, and he cries when he is hungry. One night, the father of the child made a bottle of milk for the baby, but it was too hot, and the baby wouldn't drink it. So the father added a bit of cold water, and David drank all the milk and went to sleep.

Answers to Practice Test 3

Part E – Story Retelling

Passage 3:

Freddy wanted to make a special birthday dinner for his mother. He went to the store and got everything he needed to make a nice meal, plus some extra things to make a special cake. When he was making the meal later at home, his phone rang. While talking on the phone, he forgot about the meal in the oven and it got burnt. In spite of this mishap, the special cake turned out to be delicious.

Person: Freddy

Place: store, home

Emotion or Event: his mother's birthday; makes special meal

Outcome: food burnt, but cake delicious

Sample Response 3:

It was Freddy's mother's birthday, and he really wanted to make the day special for her. He went to the store to buy the ingredients for a meal and for a birthday cake. After he had gotten home with the ingredients, his home rang and he forgot to pay attention to the food. The meal was in the oven and it got burnt, but the cake was really tasty.

Answers to Practice Test 3

Part F – Open Questions

Question 1:

Should a person ever borrow money from a family member? Please explain your opinion and give examples.

Your Opinion: no

Examples / Explanation: favors are expected

Further Information: I do not like to owe a debt.

Sample Response:

Frankly, I would never consider borrowing money from a family member. I like the freedom of knowing that I do not owe a debt to anyone, especially a family member. When a person borrows money, the person who loans the money can expect favors or special treatment from the borrower since they have extended help to them. I should add, though, that I can say this because I have a good job right now.

Useful Phrases:

<u>Frankly,</u> <u>I would never consider</u> borrowing money from a family member. <u>I like</u> the freedom of knowing that I do not owe a debt to anyone, especially a family member. When a person borrows money, the person who loans the money can expect favors or special treatment from the borrower since they have extended help to them. <u>I should add</u>, though, that <u>I can say this because</u> I have a good job right now.

Answers to Practice Test 3

Part F – Open Questions

Question 2:

Many people believe that life was more difficult a hundred years ago. Do you agree? Please explain and give examples.

Your Opinion: yes, on a physical level

Examples / Explanation: physical labor; transportation

Further Information: communication; information

Sample Response:

I believe that life was certainly more difficult a hundred years ago, at least on a physical level. Technology was not very advanced a century ago, and people had to do hard physical labor. It was also more difficult to travel, because motorized vehicles were not widely available. In addition, communicating and getting information would have also been more onerous.

Useful Phrases:

<u>I believe that</u> life was certainly more difficult a hundred years ago, <u>at least</u> on a physical level. Technology was not very advanced a century ago, and <u>people had to</u> do hard physical labor. <u>It was also</u> more difficult to travel, because motorized vehicles were not widely available. <u>In addition</u>, communicating and getting information would have also been more onerous.

Answers to Practice Test 4

Part B – Repeat

1. Just relax and try not to be nervous.

2. Could you explain the situation to me?

3. Most people really hate public speaking.

4. I can't stand it when people leave the place dirty.

5. How long does it take to get to Miami from here?

6. My short-term goal is to get an entry-level job.

7. She has worked in this lab for nearly ten years.

8. Maybe I should get to know him better, but not today.

9. I truly feel that working here has been a privilege.

10. Losing my job was one of the biggest challenges of my life.

11. Change can be frightening, but it also presents possibilities.

12. A university professor usually has several academic degrees.

13. What's the biggest worry of most people who sit down in this chair?

14. It turned out to be the best thing that ever happened.

15. That's an awful lot of responsibility on such a low salary.

16. Management reserves the right to refuse service to any customer.

Answers to Practice Test 4

Part C – Questions

1. Is a discount an increase or decrease in the price? **decrease**

2. What item would you use in the engine of your car, oil or soap? **oil**

3. If you're looking into something, are you investigating or watching?

    investigating

4. Which animal would you see at a zoo, a bear or a dinosaur? **a bear**

5. Is the North Pole cold or hot? **cold**

6. If you fail, do you do well or poorly? **poorly**

7. How many years are in a decade, ten or twenty? **ten**

8. What is longer, an inch or a mile? **a mile**

9. To examine something small, would you use a microscope or a telescope?

    a microscope

10. Which has four legs, a horse or human being? **a horse**

11. Should you do your hobby during work or your free time? **your free time**

12. There are two dogs in the house and three dogs outside. How many dogs are there? **five / There are five dogs.**

13. If someone is standoffish, are they rude or pleasant? **rude**

14. If you want an entry level job, are you just starting out or do you have experience? **starting out**

15. A person is injured in an accident. Are they an observer or a casualty? **a casualty**

16. If you greet and smile at others, are you friendly or cold? **friendly**

17. Laila is pushy. Is she assertive or quiet? **assertive**

18. Can self-starters do jobs alone or do they need help? **alone**

19. Alan has gotten away with coming to work late. Has he been punished or unnoticed? **unnoticed**

20. Why do you use a ball-point pen, to write a letter or fly an airplane? **to write a letter**

21. Brianna and Robert are inseparable. Are they close or distant? **close**

22. At a rehearsal, would you play an instrument or file a report? **play an instrument**

23. If Larry is arrogant, is he probably disliked or well-liked? **disliked**

24. By chance, you came across someone today. Did you meet them or get upset? **You meet them.**

25. Juliette is really nice to everyone. Is she amiable or forgetful? **amiable**

Answers to Practice Test 4

Part D – Sentence Builds

1. about the situation / a heads up / she gave him

   She gave him a heads up about the situation.

   Note that "heads up" means to inform someone about something in advance.

2. to find / he is struggling / the solution

   He is struggling to find the solution.

3. it seems / too much work / that she's been given

   It seems that she's been given too much work.

4. if we could / I was wondering / make it easier

   I was wondering if we could make it easier.

5. at the next meeting / will be discussed / the targets

   The targets will be discussed at the next meeting. / At the next meeting, the targets will be discussed.

6. and tasks / they could / reassess her responsibility

   The could reassess her responsibility and tasks.

7. to know / your thoughts / I'm eager

   I'm eager to know your thoughts.

8. to restore / their goal is / full services

   Their goal is to restore full services.

9. downsizing / are now / some small companies

   Some small companies are now downsizing.

10. no doubt / about that / there is

    There is no doubt about that.

Answers to Practice Test 4

Part E – Story Retelling

Passage 1:

A group of friends was playing basketball in the park, but no one had brought anything along to drink. It was a really sunny day and it was very hot, but everyone still wanted to play basketball. After about an hour, everyone got really thirsty. The nearest store was a mile away, so they decided to stop playing and everyone went home.

Person: a group of friends

Place: park

Emotion or Event: playing basketball; getting thirsty

Outcome: store far away; everyone went home

Sample Response 1:

Some friends were playing basketball in the park, but it was a very warm day, and no one had brought along anything to drink. It was a bright sunny day, so everyone felt like playing, so they played basketball for around an hour. Then everyone felt very thirsty. The store was far away, so they all decided it would be best just to go home.

Answers to Practice Test 4

Part E – Story Retelling

Passage 2:

James wanted to make pancakes for the whole family. He had the eggs, the milk, and the flour. But then he realized that he needed butter, and the store was already closed. It was getting really late and his family was hungry, so he decided to make rice and beans for everyone instead.

Person: James

Place: at home

Emotion or Event: wanted to make pancakes

Outcome: no butter; made rice and beans instead

Sample Response 2:

James felt like making pancakes for his family, so he bought the ingredients he needed, including the milk, flour, and eggs. Then he realized that he had forgotten to buy any butter. It was already late, and the store was closed. So in the end, he made rice and beans for his family instead.

Answers to Practice Test 4

Part E – Story Retelling

Passage 3:

Craig really loves going golfing. He has golfed every weekend for many years, but his friend encouraged him to try bowling instead. He went bowling every Wednesday night for a month, and he really enjoyed it. Now he goes golfing on the weekend and goes bowling every Wednesday.

Person: Craig

Place: golfing

Emotion or Event: wanted to try bowling

Outcome: now he does both

Sample Response 3:

Craig enjoyed golfing a lot, and for the past several years, he had been playing golf every weekend. A friend of his asked him if he would consider going bowling instead of golfing. Craig really enjoyed bowling, so now he also goes bowling every Wednesday evening as well.

Answers to Practice Test 4

Part F – Open Questions

Question 1:

What is the biggest personal problem that you have ever faced? Explain your answer.

Your Opinion: injured in an accident

Examples / Explanation: car accident; two months in hospital

Further Information: taught me patience and determination

Sample Response:

For me personally, the most challenging situation I ever faced was being in a serious car collision when I was younger. I had to be in the hospital for two months and had to undergo extensive physical rehabilitation. But the situation had a bright side, because it taught me a lot about patience, perseverance, and determination. These characteristics have made me the person I am today.

Useful Phrases:

<u>For me personally</u>, the most challenging situation I ever faced was being in a serious car collision when I was younger. I had to be in the hospital for two months and had to undergo extensive physical rehabilitation. But <u>the situation had a bright side</u>, because it taught me a lot about patience, perseverance, and determination. These characteristics have made me the person I am today.

Answers to Practice Test 4

Part F – Open Questions

Question 2:

Have you ever had problems with people that you live with? What kinds of problems have you had?

Your Opinion: yes, roommates

Examples / Explanation: keeping things tidy

Further Information: respecting possessions and space

Sample Response:

I am afraid to say that I had some problems living with some roommates in the past. When living space is shared, there can be conflicts and disagreements about who is going to keep the common areas tidy. Problems can also occur if a roommate does not respect another person's space or possessions. For these reasons, I would prefer to live alone or with a close family member.

Useful Phrases:

<u>I am afraid to say that</u> I had some problems living with some roommates in the past. When living space is shared, <u>there can be</u> conflicts and disagreements about who is going to keep the common areas tidy. <u>Problems can also occur if</u> a roommate does not respect another person's space or possessions. <u>For these reasons</u>, I would prefer to live alone or with a close family member.

Answers to Practice Test 5

Part B – Repeat

1. What are you waiting for?

2. It looks like everyone is gone for the day.

3. Not everyone feels the way that you do.

4. You really should hire him right now.

5. Someone will be with you shortly.

6. That's just the way she wanted it.

7. If you forget your password, click on the link below.

8. I just don't want to be the reason for the delay.

9. Mason had the last laugh.

10. How many people do you expect to attend the conference?

11. Talk to a financial advisor for information about investing.

12. One box of high-quality paper should be enough for the job.

13. The heat index declined twenty percent last year.

14. Far fewer students took a math course this term compared to last.

15. Our offices will be closed on Monday due to the holiday.

16. Protective shoes must be worn in this area at all times.

Answers to Practice Test 5

Part C – Questions

1. What's the color of the sky on a clear day? **blue**

2. The street is flooded. Is it full of cars or water? **water**

3. Does a triangle have three sides or four? **three**

4. Natalie never speaks to anyone. Is she shy or outgoing? **shy**

5. Would an oven be used to prepare food or wash clothes? **prepare food**

6. Sophie is shorter than her brother. Who is taller? **her brother / Sophie's brother**

7. Chase was thrilled about seeing his friend. Was he excited or disinterested?

    excited

8. Harrison is really witty. Is he boring or funny? **funny**

9. Valentina is clever for her age. Is she delayed or advanced? **advanced**

10. George has a broken bone. Will he get an x-ray or go for a walk? **get an x-ray**

11. If you break something by accident, have you been careless or diligent? **careless**

12. Bella's son was 4 kilograms at birth and weighed 7 kilograms a year later. How much did he gain? **three kilograms**

13. Caroline's daughter has contracted malaria. Did she become ill or get a job?

    She became ill.

14. Which is the best to drink, sea water or bottled water? **bottled water**

15. If you are a patient, are you probably in the hospital or on an airplane? **in the hospital**

16. The company wanted to re-run the advertisement. Are they repeating it or removing it? **repeating it**

17. Is cleaning the house a task or a hobby? **a task**

18. Cora is going on vacation the day after Saturday and the day before Monday. What day is she going? **Sunday / on Sunday**

19. What color is the grass? **green**

20. Do buses travel on the road or on rails? **on the road**

21. Jasper knows all of the words to the song by heart. Has he memorized them or forgotten them? **memorized them**

22. Would a mechanic use tools or a paintbrush? **tools**

23. Jason ate some candy. Did he eat something sweet or something salty? **something sweet**

24. Which is an intangible idea, love or a table? **love**

25. How many children are there in a set of twins? **two**

Answers to Practice Test 5

Part D – Sentence Builds

1. to move / is too heavy / your suitcase

    Your suitcase is too heavy to move.

2. the mistake / that she made / she regretted

    She regretted that she made the mistake. / She regretted the mistake that she made.

3. he had to / in the rain / go out

    He had to go out in the rain.

4. books about history / always enjoys / my father

    My father always enjoys books about history.

5. that mess / his mother / cleaned up

    His mother cleaned up that mess.

6. will check / the remaining files / the employees

    The employees will check the remaining files.

7. arrived late / to the meeting / our boss

    Our boss arrived late to the meeting.

8. or repaired / the broken television / will be replaced

    The broken television will be replaced or repaired.

9. along with her / she brought / her computer

    She brought her computer along with her.

10. can't stand / loud noises / he really

    He really can't stand loud noises.

Answers to Practice Test 5

Part E – Story Retelling

Passage 1:

A family was having a large new house built that had four bedrooms. The builders came to work on the house, and they put in new boards and materials every day. One day when the boss was watching over the workers, a board fell on the top of his head. He had to go to the hospital, but they did an x-ray and determined that he hadn't been injured.

Person: builders

Place: a new house

Emotion or Event: board fell on boss's head

Outcome: went to hospital, x-ray, no injury

Sample Response 1:

A company of builders was working on constructing a big new family house with four bedrooms. They worked on the house every day, and were constantly adding wood and other materials. The boss came one day to observe the workers, when a board fell onto his head. They took him to the hospital and did an x-ray, but fortunately he was not injured.

Answers to Practice Test 5

Part E – Story Retelling

Passage 2:

A mother and father lived in the city center with their two children. The children went to school every day, while the man and woman went to their jobs. The family looked forward to their vacation at the beach. When they arrived, they sunbathed, swam and built a sand castle. The older child knocked down the sand castle by accident, but they built a new one again.

Person: mother, father, two children

Place: city center

Emotion or Event: looking forward to beach vacation

Outcome: swimming, sunbathing, sand castle knocked down

Sample Response 2:

A family with a mom, dad, and two kids decided to go on vacation to a beach. They were really looking forward to it because they all were busy with their lives during the week. They arrived at the beach, and they went swimming and sunbathing. Then they built a sand castle, but the oldest child knocked it over. So they built a new one.

Answers to Practice Test 5

Part E – Story Retelling

Passage 3:

Gary wanted to make breakfast for his wife on the weekend. While his wife was still in bed, he prepared all of the food in the kitchen. Then he decided to go to the store on the corner to get some flowers. It took longer than he expected, and when he returned, she had eaten all of the food. He was a bit disappointed that she had eaten without him, but she said the food was delicious and the flowers were beautiful.

Person: Gary and his wife

Place: his house and the store

Emotion or Event: made breakfast; went to store; disappointed that she ate

Outcome: wife said food was good and flowers were nice

Sample Response 3:

Gary was going to prepare a special breakfast for his spouse one weekend. He had all of the food ready in the kitchen, when he thought it would be nice to go out to the store quickly to buy some flowers. But when he got back, she had eaten the breakfast without him, and he felt disappointed. She said the food was good, and she also really appreciated the flowers.

Answers to Practice Test 5

Part F – Open Questions

Question 1:

Should parents help their children with school work, or should children complete school work alone, without help from their parents? Please explain.

Your Opinion: alone usually, but a little help when needed

Examples / Explanation: children learn by processing information themselves

Further Information: parents can help to give an example or explanation when needed

Sample Response:

I think that it's usually best for children to do their school work alone, without the assistance of their parents. As for me, I learned best myself when I was left alone to think about and process information because that was how I figured things out. Yet, I would add that sometimes a parent may be needed to explain something or give an example to help the child on their way.

Useful Phrases:

<u>I think that</u> <u>it's usually best for</u> children to do their school work alone, without the assistance of their parents. <u>As for me</u>, I learned best myself when I was left alone to think about and process information because that was how I figured things out. <u>Yet, I would add that</u> sometimes a parent may be needed to explain something or give an example to help the child on their way.

Answers to Practice Test 5

Part F – Open Questions

Question 2:

Should all students receive an academic education or should some students be educated to do specific jobs? Please explain your opinion.

Your Opinion: academic education is not for everyone

Examples / Explanation: some people work best with their minds

Further Information: other people work with their hands

Sample Response:

In my experience, academic education, like going to a college or university, is not for everyone. For those who work best with their minds, academic education will be helpful to give them the training needed for a professional job, like accountancy or engineering. Nevertheless, other people work better with their hands and are better suited to practical or vocational jobs, like mechanical or factory work.

Useful Phrases:

<u>In my experience</u>, academic education, like going to a college or university, <u>is not for everyone</u>. <u>For those who</u> work best with their minds, academic education will be helpful to give them the training needed for a professional job, like accountancy or engineering. <u>Nevertheless</u>, other people work better with their hands and are better suited to practical or vocational jobs, like mechanical or factory work.

Answers to Practice Test 6

Part B – Repeat

1. Weren't we going to have a meeting this Friday?

2. She fell off her bike and broke her leg.

3. It's going to be windy and very rainy tomorrow.

4. Have you ever been to San Francisco?

5. It's been very hot this summer.

6. Could you please speak more loudly?

7. There were such beautiful flowers in the garden.

8. I don't like being alone because I get lonely.

9. I didn't get the promotion because I didn't have enough experience.

10. She borrowed my jacket, but never gave it back to me.

11. Advertising can be one of a company's largest expenses.

12. People really shouldn't talk about others behind their backs.

13. I wish you had told me that you weren't going to finish on time.

14. I'm thirsty. Could you get me a cold drink please?

15. I'm looking forward to the conference next month.

16. This is supposed to be a team project, so I'd like some help.

Answers to Practice Test 6

Part C – Questions

1. Which is lighter, gray or black? **gray**

2. Which is bigger, a rat or an elephant? **an elephant**

3. How many sides are in a square? **four**

4. Does a skirt cover the arms or legs? **the legs**

5. Is a broom used to clean the floor or open the door? **clean the floor**

6. Would you eat from a shoe or from a plate? **from a plate**

7. How many years are there in a century? **one hundred / a hundred**

8. Is an ambulance used for the injured or for public transportation? **for the injured**

9. If someone tells me to hold up, should I stop or continue? **stop**

10. Which one is colder, ice cream or soup? **ice cream**

11. Sophie always pays for everyone when we go out. Is she generous or stingy? **generous**

12. Does a respirator help someone breathe or eat? **breathe**

13. Which is lighter, a feather or a chair? **a feather**

14. During the day, is the desert hot or cold? **hot**

15. Does a car have four wheels or two? **four**

16. Jade is a cardiologist. Does she deal with the heart or with the feet? **with the heart**

17. The baby crawled across the floor. Was she on two feet or on her feet and hands? **feet and hands**

18. Is your mother's sister your aunt or your cousin? **your aunt**

19. How many months are there in a year? **twelve**

20. Which is more serious, an operation or an examination? **an operation**

21. Which is larger, eighty-five or sixty-three? **eighty-five**

22. What would you call the daughter of a queen? **a princess**

23. What language is spoken in Spain? **Spanish**

24. Todd was asked to fill out a form. Should he write on it or mail it? **write on it**

25. The children started to act up. Were they behaving well or badly? **badly**

Answers to Practice Test 6

Part D – Sentence Builds

1. very early / she arrived / at the party

    She arrived very early at the party. / She arrived at the party very early.

2. agree with / I completely / what you said

    I completely agree with what you said.

3. at around / he left / 5:00 o'clock

    He left at around 5:00 o'clock. / At around 5:00 o'clock, he left.

4. too exhausted / she was / to speak

    She was too exhausted to speak.

5. the shed / in the back yard / they tore down

    They tore down the shed in the back yard.

6. the prize money / that won / who was it

    Who was it that won the prize money?

7. about going ahead with / I'm not sure / the new plan

    I'm not sure about going ahead with the new plan.

8. of the company / the president / has resigned

    The president of the company has resigned.

9. go on / I need to / a special diet

    I need to go on a special diet.

10. give the letter / could you / to the receptionist

    Could you give the letter to the receptionist?

Answers to Practice Test 6

Part E – Story Retelling

Passage 1:

Steven loved to bake cake. His mother usually visited a friend on Saturday afternoon, so during that time, he had the kitchen to himself. One Saturday, he made a chocolate cake that was much larger than usual. When his mother got home, she ate a slice and said it was the best cake she had ever eaten. Then she invited the neighbors over and shared the cake with them.

Person: Steven

Place: kitchen

Emotion or Event: mother visits friend; Steven makes a big chocolate cake

Outcome: best cake ever; shared with neighbors

Sample Response 1:

Steven really enjoys baking cake. One Saturday, his mom went to visit a friend, so Steven made a large chocolate cake on his own. His mother had a piece of the cake when she got home, and said it was the best cake ever. Because the cake was so big, they gave some of it to their neighbors.

Answers to Practice Test 6

Part E – Story Retelling

Passage 2:

Billy was five years old, and he really wanted a new bicycle for his birthday. He had been telling his parents that he wanted the new bicycle, which was blue with a white stripe. His parents told him that they probably couldn't afford the new bike because it was very expensive. After looking around, his parents finally found the same bicycle second-hand for a good price. They bought it, and Billy was so happy when he got it for his birthday.

Person: Billy, 5 years old

Place: home

Emotion or Event: wanted bicycle for his birthday; parents get used bike

Outcome: Billy was happy.

Sample Response 2:

Billy was a five-year-old boy, and he really wanted a new blue and white bicycle for his birthday. His parents thought the bike was quite expensive, but they found a used one a for a good price. When they gave it to Billy on his birthday, he was really happy and excited.

Answers to Practice Test 6

Part E – Story Retelling

Passage 3:

Sarah loved to go hiking in the mountains whenever she could. She had heavy boots, warm clothing, and good walking sticks. One weekend, she decided to hike higher than she had ever gone before. She was just about to leave the trail, when she slipped and had a bad fall. She realized that she had hurt her leg, and she called for help. A man and woman helped her walk down the mountain, and she managed to drive herself to the doctor.

Person: Sarah

Place: mountains

Emotion or Event: hiking very high; fell down

Outcome: hurt her leg; got help; went to hospital

Sample Response 3:

One of Sarah's favorite pastimes was hiking in the mountains, and she had all the equipment she needed. One day, she decided to go on a hike on a very high trail, but unfortunately, she slipped, fell down, and hurt her leg. She got help from some fellow hikers, and managed to get in her car and drive to the doctor.

Answers to Practice Test 6

Part F – Open Questions

Question 1:

Some people believe that television is harmful and has no educational value. Do you agree? Why or why not?

Your Opinion: both good and bad

Examples / Explanation: documentaries and nature programs are great

Further Information: there are some poor programs

Sample Response:

There are both good and bad programs on TV nowadays. For instance, there are many documentaries that can educate the viewer about historical or scientific subjects. Furthermore, there are some very well-produced nature programs on TV from places like Africa. But it must be said that there are some very poor programs on TV also, such as reality TV and "prank" shows.

Useful Phrases:

There are both good and bad programs on TV nowadays. For instance, there are many documentaries that can educate the viewer about historical or scientific subjects. Furthermore, there are some very well-produced nature programs on TV from places like Africa. But it must be said that there are some very poor programs on TV also, such as reality TV and "prank" shows.

Answers to Practice Test 6

Part F – Open Questions

Question 2:

Imagine that you were rich and famous. Explain how your life would be different than it is now.

Your Opinion: money makes a big difference

Examples / Explanation: better house; money for family and charity

Further Information: but negative aspects, like lack of privacy

Sample Response:

There is no doubt that having money can help to solve many of life's problems. So, if I had more money, I would probably get a bigger house, and I would also give some of my money to my family and to charity. Yet, being famous is probably something that I would not like very well. I enjoy having a quiet family life, and with fame, there certainly comes celebrity and a lack of personal privacy.

Useful Phrases:

<u>There is no doubt that</u> having money can help to solve many of life's problems. <u>So, if I</u> had more money, <u>I would probably</u> get a bigger house, <u>and I would also</u> give some of my money to my family and to charity. <u>Yet</u>, being famous is probably something that I would not like very well. <u>I enjoy</u> having a quiet family life, and with fame, there certainly comes celebrity and a lack of personal privacy.

Answers to Practice Test 7

Part B – Repeat

1. You need to turn left at the fourth stoplight.

2. Her invoice was three months overdue.

3. We're going to need to come up with a better solution to this problem.

4. I was really looking for something that was higher quality.

5. The bank on the corner closed last month.

6. You can make your screen lighter or darker by pressing this button.

7. I usually have more time to myself on the weekend.

8. Bella enjoyed talking to the friends she hadn't seen in so long.

9. When you leave the room, please turn off the light.

10. I'm tired and don't really feel like going out tonight.

11. Your license is expired, so you'll need to apply for a new one.

12. The TV show that you enjoy is on at 8:30 tonight.

13. I felt terrible about forgetting to invite her.

14. He just loves hamburgers and milkshakes.

15. We really need to get that extra computer repaired.

16. You need to get the right local currency when you travel overseas.

Answers to Practice Test 7

Part C – Questions

1. Iris has gained weight. Has she become heavier or lighter? **heavier**

2. Julia is three years younger than Luis. She is 20. How old is Luis? **twenty-three**

3. Would you find a chair at a desk or in a river? **at a desk**

4. What letter comes after D and before F? **E / the letter E**

5. Is research done for science or recreation? **for science**

6. Which is usually faster, running or walking? **running**

7. What would you use to wash your hands, soap or mud? **soap**

8. Which animal can fly, a bear or a bird? **a bird**

9. Are shoes worn on the feet or the head? **the feet**

10. Which one is more fragrant, petroleum or perfume? **perfume**

11. Jackson has poor eyesight. Would he wear eyeglasses or a hearing aid? **eyeglasses**

12. Is an epidemic a health problem or a type of travel? **a health problem**

13. Eva passed up our invitation to dinner. Did she attend or decline? **decline / She declined.**

14. Would you usually find a book on a shelf or in a tree? **on a shelf**

15. Clara is a nurse. Would she work with a doctor or an architect? **a doctor**

16. Is a pizza covered with cheese or sugar? **cheese**

17. Oliver spoke abruptly to a customer. Was he rude or polite? **rude**

18. You feel exhausted. Are you tired or refreshed? **tired**

19. If it's cold outside, would you wear shorts or a coat? **a coat**

20. Alison was placated. Is she pleased or dissatisfied? **pleased**

21. Parker is fed up with his job. Is he satisfied or frustrated? **frustrated**

22. Which could be used to make a table, wood or water? **wood**

23. They had to carry on with the job. Did they continue or stop? **continue / They continued.**

24. Is the tone of a report usually informative or playful? **informative**

25. If the complaint was frivolous, was it serious or trivial? **trivial**

Answers to Practice Test 7

Part D – Sentence Builds

1. to my house / for a meal / she came

    She came to my house for a meal.

2. the assistant said / was ill / that the president

    The assistant said that the president was ill.

3. not to cry / told her / her parents

    Her parents told her not to cry.

4. was the most boring / that movie / I've ever seen

    That movie was the most boring I've ever seen.

5. this problem / talking about / let's start

    Let's start talking about this problem.

6. call me / you know the result / as soon as

    Call me as soon as you know the result.

7. our poor performance / the manager / complained about

    The manager complained about our poor performance.

8. never been / she had / there before

    She had never been there before.

9. she was nervous / to her boss / about speaking

    She was nervous about speaking to her boss.

10. everything I can / to solve the problem / I'm doing

    I'm doing everything I can to solve the problem.

Answers to Practice Test 7

Part E – Story Retelling

Passage 1:

Martha enjoyed riding her motorcycle to the ocean in her free time. She wore a helmet and always tried to be careful on the road, especially when the traffic was heavy. One day, a large truck didn't see her and pulled in front of her without looking. But Martha saw the truck in time and managed to avoid a bad accident.

Person: Martha

Place: on road with motorcycle

Emotion or Event: large truck did not see her

Outcome: she avoided an accident

Sample Response 1:

Martha loves riding her motorcycle in her free time, especially to the ocean. She was a careful, cautious driver, but one day a huge truck pulled right out in front of her without seeing her. Because of Martha's caution, she saw the truck in time and avoided an accident.

Answers to Practice Test 7

Part E – Story Retelling

Passage 2:

Thomas decided it was time to sell his parents' house since they had both passed away. Once he had made this decision, he didn't tell his brothers and sisters that he was going to sell the family home. When his oldest brother found out that the house was sold, he got very angry with Thomas. Because of this disagreement, the two brothers no longer speak to each other.

Person: Thomas

Place: parents' house

Emotion or Event: sold house; didn't tell siblings

Outcome: oldest brother was angry; doesn't speak to him

Sample Response 2:

Both of Thomas's parents had died, so he decided to sell the family home without informing any of the other siblings. However, when his oldest brother discovered this, he was very upset about what Thomas had done. Because of this, the two brothers don't speak to each other anymore.

Answers to Practice Test 7

Part E – Story Retelling

Passage 3:

Dan bought an expensive new computer that he wanted to use for college. He got the computer at a discount, so he paid a little extra for a one-year guarantee on it. After he had the computer for eight months, it didn't work anymore. He took the computer back to the store, and because he had the guarantee, they repaired it for him for free.

Person: Dan

Place: college

Emotion or Event: bought new compute on sale with guarantee

Outcome: computer broke, but he got it repaired

Sample Response 3:

Dan was about to go to college, so he needed a new computer for his school work. He wanted a rather expensive one, but he waited until it was on sale for a good price and got a one-year guarantee with it. Eight months later, the computer broke down, but Dan got it repaired for free because of the guarantee.

Answers to Practice Test 7

Part F – Open Questions

Question 1:

What are the qualities that a person should look for in a life partner? Please explain your answer and give examples.

Your Opinion: personal character

Examples / Explanation: compatibility, kindness, patience, generosity

Further Information: also important for parenthood

Sample Response:

In my opinion, personal character is the most important quality in a life partner. To spend the rest of your life with someone, the two of you need to be compatible, first of all. Besides that, I think the person's character is the most important, and I would look for someone who is kind, patient, and generous. I also hope to have children one day, so I would expect these characteristics in the mother of my children as well.

Useful Phrases:

<u>In my opinion,</u> personal character is the most important quality in a life partner. To spend the rest of your life with someone, the two of you need to be compatible, <u>first of all</u>. <u>Besides that</u>, I think the person's character <u>is the most important</u>, and I would look for someone who is kind, patient, and generous. <u>I also hope to</u> have children one day, so <u>I would expect</u> these characteristics in the mother of my children as well.

Answers to Practice Test 7

Part F – Open Questions

Question 2:

Is good health more important than having money? Please explain your answer and give examples.

Your Opinion: health is more important

Examples / Explanation: sound in mind and body

Further Information: without your life, you have nothing

Sample Response:

Without a doubt, good health is the most important thing in life, and it is definitely more important than having money. Obviously, if a person has very poor health they might die and not even be able to live the rest of their life, let alone enjoy the rest of of their life. For these reasons, I always tend to lean towards taking care of myself, so that I will hopefully have a long life and be sound in mind and body.

Useful Phrases:

<u>Without a doubt</u>, good health is the most important thing in life, <u>and it is definitely more important than</u> having money. <u>Obviously</u>, if a person has very poor health they might die and not even be able to live the rest of their life, let alone enjoy the rest of their life. <u>For these reasons</u>, <u>I always tend to lean towards</u> taking care of myself, <u>so that I will hopefully have</u> a long life and be sound in mind and body.

Answers to Practice Test 8

Part B – Repeat

1. We couldn't have finished the project without you.

2. He got a new car at that place downtown.

3. The ocean was calm, and all the stars were out.

4. He missed his flight and had to get a hotel for the night.

5. I'm afraid it doesn't feel very comfortable.

6. The Human Resources Department will make the announcement on Monday.

7. There's a ten percent discount if you pay before the fifth.

8. She enjoyed watching the people on the beach.

9. They're really looking forward to moving into their new apartment.

10. If you haven't received the order by Wednesday, please contact us.

11. You can leave your coat on the chair by the door.

12. We had been told to work late, but he decided to leave early.

13. More students are taking business studies courses than ever before.

14. I couldn't afford anything in the store, so I didn't buy anything.

15. I'll call you tomorrow to touch base with you.

16. We offer a 90-day complete-satisfaction money-back guarantee.

Answers to Practice Test 8

Part C – Questions

1. Is orange juice a liquid or a solid? **a liquid**

2. Is a lemon sweet or sour? **sour**

3. Austin managed to work things out. Did he find a solution or get a new job? **find a solution**

4. Would you cook a meal in the bedroom or the kitchen? **the kitchen**

5. Noelle felt exasperated. Was she upset or calm? **upset**

6. What month comes after September and before November? **October**

7. Is a carpet usually placed on the floor or the ceiling? **the floor**

8. Tyler is under the weather. Is he ill or on the beach? **ill / He is ill.**

9. Declan felt apprehensive about the situation. Did he have doubts or did he feel comfortable? **He had doubts.**

10. The baby warmed up to Zara after about an hour. Did the baby accept her or reject her? **accepted her / The baby accepted her.**

11. What would you use to make a dress, a sewing machine or a suitcase? **a sewing machine**

12. If something is pricey, is it expensive or inexpensive? **expensive**

13. Is a wrench used to repair something or to eat something? **repair something**

14. Arthur was reticent when asked about his opinion. Did he speak reluctantly or freely? **reluctantly**

15. You have just had an appetizing meal. Was it tasty or disgusting? **tasty / It was tasty.**

16. The interpretation of the policy was in a gray area. Was the policy strict or flexible? **flexible**

17. Amira wants to go for a hike. Will she put on boots or a swimsuit? **boots**

18. Jude was threatened with a demotion. Will he lose his job or get a lower position? **get a lower position**

19. Lilly had to deal with a disgruntled customer. Was the customer happy or dissatisfied? **dissatisfied**

20. The meeting dragged on. Did the meeting go quickly or slowly? **slowly**

21. The couple met in a secluded place. Was it private or well-traveled? **private**

22. The leaves of that flower are noxious. Are they harmful or beneficial? **harmful**

23. You want to watch a show. Would you turn on the television or open the window? **turn on the television**

24. The company decided to do away with twenty sales people. Did they hire them or fire them? **fire them**

25. Kim started to fall behind at school. Is her work delayed or accelerated? **delayed**

Answers to Practice Test 8

Part D – Sentence Builds

1. were told about / members of staff / the pay cut

   Members of staff were told about the pay cut.

2. change the information / contact human resources / in order to

   Contact human resources in order to change the information.

3. the project / on Tuesday / we'll start

   We'll start the project on Tuesday. / On Tuesday, we'll start the project.

4. get used to / he couldn't / the new schedule

   He couldn't get used to the new schedule.

5. speak to him / are you / going to

   Are you going to speak to him?

6. to wear / was too dirty / the shirt

   The shirt was too dirty to wear.

7. heard about / everyone had already / the accident

   Everyone had already heard about the accident.

8. the restaurant / on Friday / is always full

   The restaurant is always full on Friday. / On Friday, the restaurant is always full.

9. his orders / problems with / there are usually

   There are usually problems with his orders.

10. on vacation / have gone / they might

    They might have gone on vacation.

Answers to Practice Test 8

Part E – Story Retelling

Passage 1:

Stephanie had a pet rabbit that she had gotten from the pet store. She paid a lot of money for the rabbit, but after a few weeks, she realized that her pet was not well. She took the rabbit to the vet, who said that her pet had a bad stomach infection. Stephanie got some special medicine for the rabbit, and after about five days, her pet was much better.

Person: Stephanie

Place: home

Emotion or Event: pet rabbit is ill

Outcome: vet gave medicine for stomach problem; better in five days

Sample Response 1:

Stephanie had an expensive new pet rabbit that she just loved, but after she had her pet for a while, she noticed that the bunny acted like it was unwell. She took her pet to the vet, who gave it medication for a stomach infection. Stephanie gave the medicine to her pet, and it got better in five days.

Answers to Practice Test 8

Part E – Story Retelling

Passage 2:

Annie goes camping every summer with her mother and father. They especially enjoy putting the tent up at a lake near their house because they can also go swimming there. However, this summer they won't be able to camp at the lake because the road to the lake is closed. So, they are going to go to visit Annie's uncle instead.

Person: Annie

Place: campground

Emotion or Event: summer camping at lake

Outcome: road closed, staying with uncle this year

Sample Response 2:

Annie loves to go camping in the summer with her mom and dad at a lake near their house. They would usually put the tent up there and go swimming, but the road that goes to the campground is closed this year, so they can't go there. So they are going to stay with Annie's uncle this year.

Answers to Practice Test 8

Part E – Story Retelling

Passage 3:

Scott is a scientist and works for a company that investigates and explores outer space. He researches how stars are made and how they travel through space. After having worked for the company for forty years, it is now time for him to retire. He has decided to get a large telescope to use at home in his free time.

Person: Scott

Place: works at a company

Emotion or Event: researches star movement; retiring now

Outcome: got a telescope at home

Sample Response 3:

For the past forty years, Scott has been working for a company that conducts research on outer space and the movement of stars. Scott has enjoyed his work, but it is time for him to retire now. In order to pass the time, he has decided to get a new telescope so he can look at the stars at home.

Answers to Practice Test 8

Part F – Open Questions

Question 1:

Should workers get paid according to their education or their effort? Please explain your answer and give examples.

Your Opinion: both

Examples / Explanation: education is important at the start; medicine, technology

Further Information: effort and experience are also valuable for motivation

Sample Response:

My impression is that an employee's educational qualifications are important and should, of course, be reflected in the pay for a person's work. This is especially true when a person is just starting out in their career, or when continuing education is necessary in a person's area of expertise, such as jobs in medicine and technology. In addition, effort also needs to be recognized financially to motivate staff.

Useful Phrases:

<u>My impression is that</u> an employee's educational qualifications are important and should, <u>of course</u>, be reflected in the pay for a person's work. <u>This is especially true when</u> a person is just starting out in their career, or when continuing education is necessary in a person's area of expertise, <u>such as</u> jobs in medicine and technology. <u>In addition</u>, effort also needs to be recognized financially to motivate staff.

Answers to Practice Test 8

Part F – Open Questions

Question 2:

Should people give up cars and motorcycles to avoid causing pollution? Please explain your answer and give examples.

Your Opinion: not entirely

Examples / Explanation: not everyone can afford it; change must be gradual

Further Information: movement toward electric vehicles

Sample Response:

There is a great deal of talk in society nowadays about pollution and climate change, and some people have even started to drive electric vehicles for this reason. Nevertheless, this is a complicated issue because not everyone can afford to give up their car or motorcycle, not to mention affording new electric vehicles. So, giving up motorized vehicles and moving towards electric vehicles needs to be a gradual process.

Useful Phrases:

There is a great deal of talk in society nowadays about pollution and climate change, and some people have even started to drive electric vehicles for this reason. Nevertheless, this is a complicated issue because not everyone can afford to give up their car or motorcycle, not to mention affording new electric vehicles. So, giving up motorized vehicles and moving towards electric vehicles needs to be a gradual process.

Answers to Practice Test 9

Part B – Repeat

1. She always keeps her desk extremely tidy and organized.

2. It'll take him at least three more hours to arrive.

3. I have a lot of ambitions and dreams about my career.

4. Most people feel upset when they hear bad news.

5. Cleaning the house is a chore that many people would rather avoid.

6. Graduates from this college usually go on to get great jobs.

7. That decision led to a very difficult situation.

8. I'm hoping for a job with an increased level of responsibility.

9. Customers have additional rights according to applicable laws.

10. After working here for thirty years, he has decided to retire.

11. I know I should exercise more, but I don't feel like starting today.

12. I wish you could shed some light on this situation.

13. Sometimes I wish my boss would let me speak my mind.

14. My parents have given me unconditional love and support.

15. I'd really rather not locate to a new city right now.

16. Many people who walk through that door will stay here.

Answers to Practice Test 9

Part C – Questions

1. Diana felt run down. Was she cheerful or tired? **tired**

2. Would you study better in the library or the bus station? **the library**

3. The proposal floundered. Was it becoming successful or losing momentum?

    losing momentum / It was losing momentum.

4. If you're told to follow up, should you take action or do nothing? **take action**

5. Gavin wants to cut some paper. Would he use scissors or a fork? **scissors**

6. The product was out of stock. Was it available or unavailable? **unavailable**

7. How many years are in a millennium, a hundred or a thousand? **a thousand**

8. The meeting was adjourned. Did the meeting start or finish? **finish**

9. If Elise is very modest, is she humble or proud? **humble**

10. Camilla felt ecstatic. Was she excited or disappointed? **excited**

11. Which creature would you see in a forest, a snake or a dolphin? **a snake**

12. Which is greater, a kilobyte or a gigabyte? **a gigabyte**

13. To move something heavy, would you use an elevator or a ladder? **an elevator**

14. Which animal has a hump, a camel or a giraffe? **a camel**

15. Ivan was ripped off. Was he assaulted or cheated? **cheated / He was cheated.**

16. Rachel was apathetic about the job. Was she enthusiastic or indifferent?

    indifferent

17. Elliot was "in the know" about the project. Was he knowledgeable or ignorant?

    knowledgeable / He was knowledgeable.

18. The teacher spoke to the boisterous children. Were the children noisy or clever?

    noisy

19. The plans for the new office fell through. Did the plans fail or proceed? **fail /**

    The plans failed.

20. The company discovered an irregularity. Was the discovery probably surprising

    or expected? **surprising**

21. Myla has one shirt on the chair and three shirts on the bed. How many shirts are

    there? **four shirts / There are four shirts.**

22. The employees were asked to assemble at three o'clock. Are they going to leave

    or get together? **get together**

23. A customer is getting agitated on the phone. Is the customer appreciative or

    distressed? **distressed**

24. Leo wanted to get back at Brandon. Is Leo going to get revenge or say "thank

    you"? **get revenge**

25. The employees were asked to get behind the new plan. Were the employees

    asked to support or reject the plan? **support / support it / support the plan**

Answers to Practice Test 9

Part D – Sentence Builds

1. your opinion / to hear / I want

    I want to hear your opinion

2. greatly increase / they hope to / their profits

    They hope to greatly increase their profits.

3. about the plan / more information / I gave her

    I gave her more information about the plan.

4. the manager said / more tasks / that we will be given

    The manager said that we will be given more tasks.

5. could we / the meeting / possibly reschedule

    Could we possibly reschedule the meeting?

6. finally found / he has / the solution

    He has finally found the solution.

7. that it actually / I doubt / happened that way

    I doubt that it actually happened that way.

8. next Monday / will be discussed / the change in hours

    The change in hours will be discussed next Monday. / Next Monday, the change in hours will be discussed.

9. reduce and reallocate / they need to / her responsibilities

    They need to reduce and reallocate her responsibilities.

10. to expand / are trying / some companies

    Some companies are trying to expand.

Answers to Practice Test 9

Part E – Story Retelling

Passage 1:

Jane works as a professor at a university teaching English to international students. She teaches English speaking skills and helps students prepare for exams. She really enjoys her job, especially meeting new people from different cultures and helping them improve their communication skills. The students really appreciate her hard work and attention.

Person: Jane, English teacher

Place: university

Emotion or Event: helps students prepare for exams; enjoyment

Outcome: students like her

Sample Response 1:

Jane is an English teacher at a university. She teaches English speaking and exam skills to students from abroad, and she really enjoys meeting them, helping them improve their English, and finding out about their cultures. The students really like her and appreciate her dedication.

Answers to Practice Test 9

Part E – Story Retelling

Passage 2:

When Adam was born, his legs didn't work properly. As he got older, he learned how to use a wheelchair. He also learned how to swim and became the best swimmer on the team at school. He won many swimming competitions and began to train for the Olympics. Last year, he was awarded an Olympic gold medal for his country in swimming.

Person: Adam, problem with legs

Place: Olympics

Emotion or Event: swimming competitions and training

Outcome: won gold medal

Sample Response 2:

Adam was born with a problem with his legs, and he needed to use a wheelchair. When he got into school, he started to swim and was the best swimmer on the school team. He worked hard at training and competitions, and went to the Olympics. He won a gold medal in swimming last year for his country's team.

Answers to Practice Test 9

Part E – Story Retelling

Passage 3:

Debbie had just graduated from high school and was looking forward to going to college. She worked hard all summer and had earned enough money to rent a large apartment at college with some of her friends. But two of her friends didn't earn enough money to pay their share of the rent. So, in the end, Debbie had to get a smaller apartment.

Person: Debbie

Place: college apartment

Emotion or Event: wanted to share apartment with friends

Outcome: two friends couldn't pay; she got smaller place

Sample Response 3:

Debbie had just finished high school and was getting ready to go to college. She got a summer job to earn enough money to rent an apartment with some other students. In the end, a couple of her friends didn't have enough money to pay the rent, though, so Debbie had to rent a smaller place.

Answers to Practice Test 9

Part F – Open Questions

Question 1:

Is a university education important in order to get ahead at work? Please explain your answer and give examples.

Your Opinion: not always

Examples / Explanation: business and real-world experience are also important

Further Information: depends on type of job

Sample Response:

My point of view is that a university education is not always necessary in order to advance in the workplace. In most situations, a large amount of learning takes place on the job, and there is certainly no substitute for the real-world experience of carrying out the daily tasks for one's work. Yet, this depends on the work being performed. For instance, university professors usually must have academic degrees for their jobs.

Useful Phrases:

<u>My point of view is that</u> a university education <u>is not always necessary</u> in order to advance in the workplace. <u>In most situations</u>, a large amount of learning takes place on the job, and <u>there is certainly no substitute for</u> the real-world experience of carrying out the daily tasks for one's work. <u>Yet, this depends on</u> the work being performed. <u>For instance</u>, university professors usually must have academic degrees for their jobs.

Answers to Practice Test 9

Part F – Open Questions

Question 2:

Should parents punish their children for being naughty? Please explain your answer and give examples.

Your Opinion: yes

Examples / Explanation: helps children learn from mistakes; reinforces good behavior

Further Information: taking away privileges, rather than physical punishment

Sample Response:

I have no doubt that punishing children helps then to learn from their mistakes and also reinforces good and responsible behavior. When I was a child, I would be told that I couldn't go to a party, for example, if I disobeyed my parents. Taking away privileges like this makes a child think about what they have done. However, I should also mention that I am opposed to any physical punishment, like spanking.

Useful Phrases:

<u>I have no doubt that</u> punishing children helps then to learn from their mistakes and also reinforces good and responsible behavior. When I was a child, I would be told that I couldn't go to a party, <u>for example</u>, if I disobeyed my parents. Taking away privileges <u>like this</u> makes a child think about what they have done. <u>However</u>, <u>I should also mention that</u> I am opposed to any physical punishment, like spanking.

Answers to Practice Test 10

Part B – Repeat

1. Thanks for waiting so patiently for me to get approval.

2. I don't have any more information at the present time.

3. He stood there like he was waiting for someone.

4. Good communication skills are essential for jobs in customer service.

5. Everyone at the company is entitled to an extra day of vacation this year.

6. I'm sorry for the inconvenience you've had from this situation.

7. There are simply no excuses for not finishing the job on time.

8. She had high hopes about getting the job.

9. Several staff members failed to attend the meeting.

10. Can you please put some more paper in the copier?

11. If you could hold the line, I'll get right back to you.

12. I'm afraid we can't accommodate your request at this time.

13. The ink was too light, and I couldn't read the document.

14. Their prices went up by seven percent last year.

15. If you don't comply with the instructions, you could be fined.

16. He's out of the office, but he'll be back on Thursday.

Answers to Practice Test 10

Part C – Questions

1. The car changed hands. Was it repaired or sold? **sold / It was sold.**

2. Would a teacher usually work at a college or a factory? **at a college**

3. Which color is brighter, yellow or brown? **yellow**

4. The rain finally let up. Did it stop or get worse? **stop / It stopped.**

5. How many items are there in a dozen? **twelve**

6. Kevin was excluded from the team. Did he play the game or stay at home? **stay at home**

7. Does a rectangle have three sides or four? **three / three sides**

8. The manager told Adelle to get her act together. Was she being scolded or complimented? **scolded**

9. Nick is going to repair the roof of his house. Will he probably need a hammer or a bucket? **a hammer**

10. Elaina is heavier than her brother. Who weighs more? **Elaina**

11. Is playing computer games a pastime or a chore? **a pastime**

12. What season comes after spring and before autumn? **summer / the summer**

13. Charlie went back on his promise. Did he keep his promise or break his promise? **break his promise / He broke his promise.**

14. The conference was extremely dull. Was it boring or interesting? **boring / It was boring.**

15. Brooke made the suggestion out of the blue. Was her suggestion anticipated or unexpected? **unexpected**

16. There was a discrepancy in their claims. Did they agree or disagree? **disagree**

17. Jesse was skeptical about the plan. Did he have doubts or was he certain? **He had doubts.**

18. Danielle decided to speak up about the situation. Did she give her opinion or tell a story? **give her opinion**

19. If Tristan gave a coherent speech, was he understood or confusing? **understood / He was understood.**

20. The two companies are adversaries. Do they compete or cooperate with each other? **compete with each other**

21. If you are a witness to a crime, did you see something or get hurt? **see something**

22. Emilio wanted to compose himself. Was he trying to get excited or calm down? **calm down**

23. Which one is usually luxurious, first-class or second-class? **first-class**

24. Caden had to take a back seat on the project. Is he going to have more responsibility or less responsibility? **less responsibility**

25. Anna wants to make up with Jane after their disagreement. Should Anna apologize to her or ignore her? **apologize / apologize to her / apologize to Jane**

Answers to Practice Test 10

Part D – Sentence Builds

1. bake cakes / loves to / my mother

   My mother loves to bake cakes.

2. for the damage / his sister / was blamed

   His sister was blamed for the damage.

3. to work late / will need / all team members

   All team members will need to work late.

4. a huge discount / offered us / the salesperson

   The salesperson offered us a huge discount.

5. to bring / she forgot / her notes

   She forgot to bring her notes.

6. not to eat / he was told / at his desk

   He was told not to eat at his desk.

7. for the item / a refund / will be offered

   A refund for the item will be offered. / A refund will be offered for the item.

8. to fit the space / is too large / the table

   The table is too large to fit the space.

9. that she had made / she hadn't realized / a mistake

   She hadn't realized that she had made a mistake.

10. was canceled / the picnic / because of the rain

    The picnic was canceled because of the rain.

Answers to Practice Test 10

Part E – Story Retelling

Passage 1:

Louise is a gardener who has her own gardening business. In the morning, she sells plants and flowers at her store, and in the afternoon, she goes to other people's homes to do their gardening. Sometimes other people ask her to put new plants and flowers in their gardens, but usually she just trims the flowers and clears things up for them.

Person: Louise, gardener

Place: store and gardens

Emotion or Event: goes to other people's homes

Outcome: plants flowers or tidies up

Sample Response 1:

Louise has her own business, working as a gardener. She has a store, where she works selling things in the morning, and she also goes to people's homes in the afternoons. She sometimes plants flowers and plants for other people, but more often than not, she just tidies things up for them in their gardens.

Answers to Practice Test 10

Part E – Story Retelling

Passage 2:

Janet was going on a long vacation to Australia, and she realized she needed to buy a new suitcase. She looked at suitcases at a lot of stores, and finally decided to get one that was made of cloth and closed with a zipper. However, when she packed her suitcase for the trip, it was too full and the zipper broke. So, she had to borrow a suitcase from her friend instead.

Person: Janet

Place: stores

Emotion or Event: vacation to Australia; shopping for new suitcase

Outcome: buys suitcase with zipper; it breaks; borrows suitcase from friend

Sample Response 2:

Janet was going to take a vacation to Australia, so she wanted to get a new suitcase for her trip. She went shopping for one and visited many stores. Then she finally found one with a zipper and decided to buy it. However, when she was packing it at home, the zipper on the suitcase broke. In the end, she borrowed a suitcase from a friend instead.

Answers to Practice Test 10

Part E – Story Retelling

Passage 3:

Henry had worked hard to prepare for an English test he needed to take in order to apply for his job. He looked at recordings and videos on the internet, and even bought a special book to help him study. After he finished his test, he was told that he got the highest test score that the company had ever seen. The company hired him, and he has been promoted to manager.

Person: Henry

Place: company

Emotion or Event: English test for new job; studied hard

Outcome: got highest score ever; got hired and promoted

Sample Response 3:

Henry needed to take an English test for a job that he was applying for. He worked really hard getting ready for it, using recordings, a book, and the internet. When he had taken his exam, the company told him that he had received the best test score ever. He got hired by the company, and later got promoted to a management position.

Answers to Practice Test 10

Part F – Open Questions

Question 1:

Children should take care of their elderly parents. Do you agree? Please explain your answer and give examples.

Your Opinion: yes

Examples / Explanation: parents care for us as children; they make sacrifices

Further Information: older parents need help – financial or live-in

Sample Response:

I agree that children should help to take care of their parents as they age. Our parents do an awful lot for us when we are small. A good parent will make sacrifices to care for their children and always wants the best for them. In the same way, a good child should help his or her older parents. This might mean contributing financially to a parent's care with the help of one's siblings, or even having a parent live with a child in some cases.

Useful Phrases:

<u>I agree that</u> children should help to take care of their parents as they age. Our parents do an awful lot for us when we are small. A good parent will make sacrifices to care for their children and always wants the best for them. <u>In the same way,</u> a good child should help his or her older parents. <u>This might mean</u> contributing financially to a parent's care with the help of one's siblings, or even having a parent live with a child <u>in some cases</u>.

Answers to Practice Test 10

Part F – Open Questions

Question 2:

It's impossible to have a job and study for college at the same time. Do you agree? Please explain your answer and give examples.

Your Opinion: yes

Examples / Explanation: takes hard work, organization, dedication

Further Information: more difficult with a family

Sample Response:

I agree with the opinion that it is possible to have a job and attend classes at the same time, although doing so requires hard work, organization, and dedication. In fact, I myself am attending college in the evening and working during the day. It isn't too difficult for me now because I am single, but I realize that it would be much more difficult if I had family commitments.

Useful Phrases:

<u>I agree with the opinion that</u> it is possible to have a job and attend classes at the same time, <u>although doing so</u> requires hard work, organization, and dedication. <u>In fact,</u> I myself am attending college in the evening and working during the day. It isn't too difficult for me now because I am single, <u>but I realize that it</u> would be much more difficult <u>if I had</u> family commitments.

www.ingramcontent.com/pod-product-compliance
Lightning Source LLC
Chambersburg PA
CBHW081752100526
44592CB00015B/2395